THE GIFT

OF THE

CROSS

THE GIFT
OF THE
CROSS

LENTEN REFLECTIONS
IN THE
HOLY CROSS TRADITION

Edited by
ANDREW GAWRYCH, C.S.C.

ave maria press AmP notre dame, indiana

© 2009 by Priests of Holy Cross, Indiana Province

All rights reserved. No part of this book may be used or reproduced in any manner whatsoever, except in the case of reprints in the context of reviews, without written permission from Ave Maria Press®, Inc., P.O. Box 428, Notre Dame, IN 46556.

Founded in 1865, Ave Maria Press is a ministry of the Indiana Province of Holy Cross.

www.avemariapress.com

ISBN-10 1-59471-202-6   ISBN-13 978-1-59471-202-9

Cover and text design by John R. Carson.

Cover photo © Jim Zuckerman/Corbis.

Printed and bound in the United States of America.

INTRODUCTION

☧

To bear the Cross as a gift—it sounds like an outrageous, even irresponsible way to live. Jesus quite clearly tells us to pick up our cross and follow him, and so we all must bear the cross given us in our lives. But we endure crosses; we do not bear them as gifts. That, at least, is what we tend to think.

We in the religious family of Holy Cross, however, believe that the Cross can be borne as a gift. After all, it is only from the Cross of Christ that all creation has received the unparalleled gift of salvation. Blessed Basil Moreau, the founder of the priests, brothers, and sisters of Holy Cross, realized this truth and established it as the community's motto: *Ave Crux, Spes Unica*, "Hail the Cross, Our Only Hope."

Since our founding in France in 1837, we have sought to bring the good news of our hope in the Cross to schools, universities, parishes, and other ministries on five continents; for when we see the Cross as our only hope, we begin to discover how even the Cross can be borne as a gift, the gift of our salvation.

In the season of Lent, the Church enters into the mystery of Christ's Cross in a unique and purposeful way. Through our Lenten disciplines of prayer, fasting, and almsgiving, and through our acts of penance, we seek to unite ourselves ever more closely and intimately with the saving mystery that is the Cross.

As the season of the Cross, however, Lent is also the season of our hope. And through the reflections of this book, we in Holy Cross seek to cultivate in others the great hope of this season by testifying to the hope we have found in the Cross in our lives and ministry.

Along the way, other major themes of our Holy Cross tradition also emerge from the reflections. They include our trust in Divine Providence, our familial spirit and unity, our eucharistic fellowship and worship, our belief that education is both of the mind and the heart, and our apostolic zeal to make God known, loved, and served.

The reflections, written by Holy Cross priests, brothers, and sisters from around the world, begin on Ash Wednesday and continue through the Triduum to the Easter Octave, during which the Church celebrates the day of the Lord's Resurrection—the goal of our Lenten journey—for eight consecutive days. Each reflection begins with a quotation from the scripture readings for the day. The Sunday readings come from Cycle A. The reflections are meant to be read—ideally alongside the daily scripture readings—as part of personal, familial, or communal prayer and meditation each day.

Our prayer is that these reflections will enrich and deepen your Lenten journey toward the joy and new life of Easter, so that through the course of these holy days you will come to believe with those of us in Holy Cross: There is no failure the Lord's love cannot reverse, no humiliation he cannot exchange for blessing, no anger he cannot dissolve, no routine he cannot transfigure. All is swallowed up in the victory of his Cross. Our crucified and risen Lord has nothing but gifts to offer. It remains only for us to find how even the Cross can be borne as a gift.

Andrew Gawrych, C.S.C.

Ash Wednesday

Yet even now, says the Lord, return to me with all your heart, with fasting, with weeping, and with mourning; rend your hearts and not your clothing. Return to the Lord, your God.

—Joel 2:12–13

MAISIE WAS A developmentally impaired woman in her sixties who volunteered at the parish office. She loved stuffing envelopes and inserting pages in the parish bulletin. Those were her "jobs." At every visit, Maisie would come by my office to ask, "Are you my friend, Fr. Milt?" After I'd smile and nod yes, she would go off to report to everyone: "Fr. Milt is my friend."

What we do in Lent is to renew our "jobs" and our friendship with the One who gives us the strength for them. No matter what we do, our jobs are ultimately simple and familiar: loving God above all, and loving our neighbor as ourselves. But over time we grow neglectful in fulfilling them from busyness, selfishness, weariness. We also forget the One who has invited us to work with him. So we need to work again at prayer, self-awareness, and generosity. We need to ask again if Jesus is our Friend, so that in seeing him smile and nod yes to us, we can return to our jobs—making God known, loved, and served—with hearts renewed.

Milt Adamson, C.S.C.

Thursday after Ash Wednesday

"If any want to become my followers, let them deny themselves and take up their cross daily and follow me. For those who want to save their life will lose it, and those who lose their life for my sake will save it."

—Luke 9:23–24

AT THE HEART of Lent is the doctrine of the Cross. The Cross is also at the heart of our Holy Cross tradition, incorporated into our motto and symbol. It is a difficult doctrine to embrace, but we in Holy Cross proclaim that the Cross can, in fact, be borne as a gift. We believe this because we have witnessed it in our lives and in the lives of others. We have seen how our fellow religious have embraced it even amidst an addiction to alcohol, thus finding God's healing strength not only to lead them forward, but also to give others the hope they need to bear similar crosses. We have stood by parents at their child's deathbed as they have made the compassionate decision to share their child's organs so that another child might live.

The special grace of this season is to strengthen our resolve to embrace the Cross no matter what form it takes in our lives. We do so confident that there is no failure the Lord's love cannot reverse, no humiliation he cannot exchange for blessing. All is swallowed up in victory; all is swallowed up in new life.

George C. Schmitz, C.S.C.

Friday after Ash Wednesday

Is not this the fast I choose: to loose the bonds of injustice, to undo the thongs of the yoke, to let the oppressed go free, and to break every yoke?

—Isaiah 58:6

MANY PEOPLE THINK that we religious make a big sacrifice by not having a family, and that is true. But that sacrifice and the other sacrifices we make free and empower us to serve and help others. In my case, it frees and empowers me to work with the children in the neighborhoods of Guadalupe, Mexico, children like Bryant who live in houses with dirt floors, makeshift walls and roofs, and no hot water. And that is why I became a sister, to teach and work with poor children so that they could have a better life.

Lent is the season of making sacrifices, yet we do not make sacrifices simply for their own sake. We make sacrifices precisely so that we can be freed and empowered to love God more by helping our brothers and sisters. In this regard, Lent is really the season of doing things for others. During these forty days, we must ask ourselves if we are truly doing all we can to help those in need. Reaching out to the poor and suffering will require great sacrifices of us, but they are worth it, for those are the sacrifices God so desires.

Michelle Toepp, C.S.C.

Saturday after Ash Wednesday

"Why do you eat and drink with tax collectors and sinners?" Jesus answered, "Those who are well have no need of a physician, but those who are sick; I have come to call not the righteous but sinners to repentance."

—Luke 5:30–32

I CONFRONT MY own stereotypes of others every day. My ministry among the marginalized in downtown Portland opens me to the authentic stories of suffering people. I let go of my prejudice that the homeless are lazy when I hear the story of Joe who suffers from stifling depression because his father sexually abused him. The label of drunkard falls away when Betty confesses to me she turned to alcohol and drugs when she witnessed her father kill her mother. The tag of mental illness is ripped off when I befriend Paul, who teaches me how to be honest in prayer.

Jesus called tax collectors and sinners around him because they were marginalized from their communities. He turned the tables on who was labeled "sinner"—a category where I find myself when my ignorance hides behind prejudice and discrimination. People on the margins peel away our stereotypes and false identities so that we cling to God with raw love. Their vulnerability teaches us a new acceptance of all who long for hope.

Ronald Patrick Raab, C.S.C.

Sunday, Week One

Then Jesus was led up by the Spirit into the wilderness to be tempted by the devil.

—Matthew 4:1

WITHIN THE SPRAWLING parish of El Señor de la Esperanza in Lima, Peru there is an area that, as it grew, took on the name *la Boca del Diablo* (the Devil's Mouth). Stories are told of strangers who entered this violent and menacing place never to return. The first parish chapel built there was burned to the ground by those hostile to the holy intrusion. The second chapel stands on that same spot. As if to imitate the bold move to build again, and perhaps relieved that someone had faced the devil, the residents began to refer to their neighborhood as *la Mano de Dios* (the Hand of God), and so it is called today.

We all have devils in our lives we must face with courage and faith, armed with the assurance that the mouth of the devil is no match for the hand of our God. And the most challenging devil is the one whose temptations fascinate us most.

The same Spirit who led Jesus into the desert invites us, if we are inclined to be so bold, to follow where we might not normally want to go, where we will find ourselves face-to-face with our own fascination with pleasure, wealth, and power. And our sojourn into that wilderness can be as purposeful as Jesus' forty days to face the devil. But we do not go to the wilderness to stay there, to keep the temptations at bay. Rather, we let ourselves be led into the wilderness by the Spirit in order to know our devils better so that we can then return to where they are, but this time less captivated by them. To overcome the temptations that fascinate so many in our world is a prophetic witness we so desperately need.

Don Fetters, C.S.C.

Monday, Week One

"Lord, when was it that we saw you hungry and gave you food, or thirsty and gave you something to drink?" . . . *"Truly I tell you, just as you did it to one of the least of these who are members of my family, you did it to me."*

—Matthew 25:37–40

IF JESUS WERE here in the flesh, if he were hungry, naked, or distressed, it would be so easy—even pleasurable—to rush to attend to him. Who of us would refuse Jesus? But at my ministry with the homeless at André House, I see people who are dirty, cranky, not always appreciative, and quite often high on alcohol or drugs. Why is it so hard to reach out to these people day after day? I believe it's because we do not take this directive from Jesus seriously enough. For us to reach out continually to the homeless, the poor, and the needy, we have to refrain from thinking, "That's just Gloria or Willy looking for another handout." If we instead think, "Look, it's Jesus, and he's in need," then we wouldn't think twice, no matter how often it was asked of us. Of all the passages that refer to Jesus, this is one meant to be taken literally. It's that simple: When we serve our sisters and brothers in need, we are really serving Jesus. And how can we refuse Jesus?

Bill Wack, C.S.C.

Tuesday, Week One

As the rain and the snow come down from heaven, and do not return there until they have watered the earth, making it bring forth and sprout . . . so shall my word be that goes out from my mouth.

—Isaiah 55:10–11

THE HEAVY DOWNPOUR came right on God's cue. We were in the fifth reading of the Easter Vigil at St. Brendan Parish in Kitete, Tanzania: "As the rain and snow come down from heaven . . . ." With our corrugated roof and no ceiling, the rain was deafening. The reader raised his voice to the maximum, but only a few in the front could barely hear him. Yet even as the people strained to hear, smiles of joy came across their faces. The farms were well prepared by this time, only waiting for this blessed rain to water them so the wheat could be sown and new life bloom again.

That downpour and the growth it would sprout were a perfect image of what God had done for us that Lent. God had showered us with the blessings of his word, and we were entering Easter blooming anew with his life. And that is the hope for all of us every Lent. We hope through our Lenten practices, especially the daily reading of scripture, that the Lord will pour his word upon us. We do so trusting that God's word always accomplishes its purpose: our salvation.

David Eliaona, C.S.C.

Wednesday, Week One

*Create in me a clean heart, O God, and
put a new and right spirit within me.*
　　　　　　　　　　—Psalm 51:10–11

OCCASIONALLY, I SUGGEST that students in
my residence hall give up beer for Lent. There
are no laughs or chuckles, perhaps a few looks
of horror. Candy or desserts are fine, but
cutting out beer is a drastic step for a college
sophomore. Perhaps they're right. Lent is a
new beginning, not an ultimate resolution to
our struggles. Prodigals who have wandered far
from God may require a lightning bolt epipha-
ny, but mostly, spiritual progress is like exercise.
Going from couch potato to marathoner takes
time, and we need to be patient and persevere
through our off days. By graduation many of
the students who arrived four years earlier like
lost sheep in new pastures have undergone
a transformation. Those changes are effected
unevenly and sometimes painfully. They are
usually gradual in pace. There is not one of us
who can't do just a little more and walk a few

steps farther with the Lord each day. Like zeal-
ous gardeners dutifully working on their patch
each day, we continue cultivating and tending
our hearts, motivated by small sprouts of suc-
cess to bring our lives to fullest bloom.

James B. King, C.S.C.

Thursday, Week One

*"Ask, and it will be given you; search,
and you will find; knock, and the door
will be opened for you. For everyone
who asks receives, and everyone who
searches finds, and for everyone who
knocks, the door will be opened."*

—Matthew 7:7–8

DO WE REALLY believe that God answers our
prayers? After all, Jesus says to ask and it will
be given to us, to search and we will find. If we
get the feeling at times that God does not hear
us, perhaps it is because we limit our prayer to
petition and neglect prayer of praise, thanksgiving, and repentance. We might feel like the

first-grader who told her mom, "I don't believe there is a God!" After some gentle probing, the mom discovered that her daughter prayed for grandma to get better, yet she died. Then she prayed for a puppy for her birthday, but no little dog came. And so the girl concluded there was no God.

There are definitely times when I feel that way, asking, "Where are you God?" But other times, especially when I am praying for the Spirit's guidance and offering God praise and thanksgiving, the answer just pops up, often in the most unexpected way. Our God is a God of surprises, and so while the answer to our prayers is often what we least expect, it is always what we need.

Jean Goulet, C.S.C.

Friday, Week One

"When you are offering your gift at the altar, if you remember that your brother or sister has something against you, leave your gift there before the altar and go; first be reconciled to your brother or sister, and then come and offer your gift."

—Matthew 5:23–24

I AMAZE MYSELF sometimes, but not in a good way. When wronged, I am often tempted to hold on to the hurt and wallow in self-pity. I'm certainly not proud of it. It makes this teaching of Jesus very uncomfortable to hear, let alone put into practice. I always expect Jesus to say that if I have something against my brother or sister, then I must go and apologize. That's natural; that's acceptable. I am able to apologize.

Jesus, however, is saying something quite different. He is saying that if someone has something against *me*, then I must go and be the reconciler. I must let go of the temptation to close in on myself and instead go out to the other and seek reconciliation first. That goes against the grain of how we normally live out our relationships, yet Jesus calls all of us who come to him to have hearts that love and forgive. And so if we are to approach him with the gift of ourselves, we first must approach our brothers and sisters with the gift of ourselves in humility and love.

Thomas A. Dziekan, C.S.C.

Saturday, Week One

"I say to you, Love your enemies and pray for those who persecute you, so that you may be children of your Father in heaven."

—Matthew 5:44–45

I LIVE IN Canada, a country where I have no fear of persecution. I'm not aware of any "real enemies." Yet in community life and in ministry, there are individuals who tax my patience or are a challenge for me. Sometimes it's people who love to control or manipulate. Other times, it's those who are overly demanding or never seem satisfied. Still other times it's simply people who do not seem to understand me. Our Holy Cross Constitutions describe this reality well when they speak of how faults and shortcomings will make us each a trial to others from time to time.

Every Lent we are presented anew with this gospel challenge to act as Jesus would act: to love and to pray for these individuals. Some days, that can seem as daunting as loving enemies or persecutors. From my many Lenten journeys I have come to recognize the wisdom of Jesus' call to change and do my best to be reconciled. I also give thanks for those who see me as a challenge and are able to follow his admonition to love and to pray for me. For it is only when we all live as children of our Father in heaven that we become true sisters and brothers to one another.

John Vickers, C.S.C.

Sunday, Week Two

*Jesus took with him Peter and James
and his brother John and led them up a
high mountain, by themselves. And he
was transfigured before them, and his
face shone like the sun, and his clothes
became dazzling white.*

—Mathew 17:1–2

IT IS A special moment when someone comes
to our door asking to join Holy Cross. As director of formation for our men's community in
Mexico, I interview these young adults. Having
great respect for the relationship with God that
brought them to us, I also hint there is more
to come. One of them, who came knocking
years ago, recently presented his request to
make final vows. It was inspiring to read his
petition describing the action of God that has
transformed his heart and soul. In a way, he
is the same person. In a way, he is a person
profoundly transformed. Like the athlete who
finds his game only after years of disciplined
training, like the diamond that reflects the

light only after being cut by the jeweler, he has become a man of God for others.

And yet his growth, like the growth of all of us, remains incomplete, for our transformation into Christ is never finished. There is always more to come. That is why the Church gives us another Lent. It is not that our Lenten practices of prayer, fasting, and almsgiving themselves transform us, but that they open our hearts and minds anew to the grace of conversion. With this openness and an eye toward grace, all the moments that make up our daily lives—from the joyful to the sorrowful, from the amazing to the routine—can become gifts of the divine jeweler, transforming us into more brilliant reflections of his love. It is then that the glory of the transfiguration will be seen in the glimmering transformation of our lives into his.

Tom Zurcher, C.S.C.

Monday, Week Two

"Give, and it will be given to you. A good measure, pressed down, shaken together, running over, will be put into your lap; for the measure you give will be the measure you get back."

—Luke 6:38

MY FIRST MISSION was as a catechist in a tribal village in Bangladesh. I used to go there during the week to teach and then on Sundays to lead prayer. The village was seven miles from the convent on a dirt road through the forest. Other than walking, the only means of travel was cycling. When the sun was hot or it rained, I was tempted not to go, but the thought of depriving the students of learning or the people of getting together to pray pushed me to make the hard trip. On every visit their joyous welcome overwhelmed me and made me forget my pain. The villagers' faith and trust in Divine Providence touched my core. Even in their poverty, they were happy and generous. Their love nourished me to become a better person and deepen my faith. I was truly given more than what I gave.

In today's broken world, we are challenged by Jesus to accept and share our giftedness. It might be hard; our selfishness and personal interest may stand in our way. But when we open our hearts and share our treasures, we experience God's love in abundance.

Pushpa Gomes, C.S.C.

Tuesday, Week Two

Though your sins are like scarlet, they shall be like snow; though they are red like crimson, they shall become like wool.

—Isaiah 1:18

THE IMAGE WAS unforgettable—Pope John Paul II huddled in a cell with Mehmet Ali Agca, his would-be assassin, in a dramatic act of reconciliation. The poignant picture was broadcast across the globe because in a seemingly unforgiving world, such unconditional forgiveness can only be of God. That powerful but brief encounter gave us hope that if one man can show such profound forgiveness, then God's mercy must be so much stronger. Though our sins may be like scarlet, with God's benevolence they can become like snow.

In my own times of sinfulness, I have found great comfort in the witness of our founder, Blessed Basil Moreau. Moreau was no stranger to humiliation and betrayal; he suffered tremendous injustices in his life. Like Pope John Paul II, however, he recognized the transformative power of God's mercy. If these men can humbly seek reconciliation with their offenders, so too must God faithfully seek us in our own sinful transgressions, but with even more love and intensity. All we need do is welcome that gift.

Paul Bednarczyk, C.S.C.

Wednesday, Week Two

"Whoever wishes to be great among you must be your servant, and whoever wishes to be first among you must be your slave; just as the Son of Man came not to be served but to serve, and to give his life a ransom for many."

—Matthew 20:26–28

I ALWAYS WANTED to serve the people of God. I never thought of being president of Notre Dame, nor did I want to be. I was happy being a dorm rector and professor. Then, next thing I knew, I was executive vice-president and then, three years later, president. It just happened. Yet whatever happens in our lives, wherever we find ourselves, there is no calling in life that cannot be put in God's service.

The way we put our lives in God's service— whether teaching classes, flying airplanes, or raising children—is to belong to the people God brings into our lives. That is what Jesus did. He belonged to the people his Father brought into his life, and thus the poor, the downtrodden, and the outcast all felt they could make a claim on Jesus and his love. As his disciples, we are called to belong to others as Jesus did, so that they, too, can make a claim on our love. In this way, our lives bring the hope of salvation to others and become prayers in service of our Heavenly Father.

Theodore M. Hesburgh, C.S.C.

Thursday, Week Two

Blessed are those who trust in the Lord. . . . They shall be like a tree planted by water, sending out its roots by the stream. It shall not fear when heat comes, and its leaves shall stay green.

—Jeremiah 17:7–8

I KNEW AN old monk with a wrinkled face and gnarled hands, but whose eyes were bright and whose words were always encouraging. He had been passed over several times for positions of responsibility in the abbey. "God called me to be a monk, not an abbot," he would say with a sparkle in his eye. I knew a seminarian whose health failed just as he was to enter the Holy Cross novitiate. He lived in hospice for over a year, yet was allowed to profess his vows by special indult. He kept a long list of people to pray for each day. "This is my ministry," he would say with satisfaction. I knew a widow whose ten children testify to her steadfast faith. "She was always there for us, and only when we were older did we know what dad's death had cost her." "You are my reward," she would tell them.

These three friends, unexceptional in almost every way, showed me how blessed are those who trust in the Lord and his providence. The heat came; their leaves stayed green. That is no small matter, yet our hope is to do the same.

James Lackenmier, C.S.C.

Friday, Week Two

"I tell you, the kingdom of God will be taken away from you and given to a people that produces the fruits of the kingdom."

—Matthew 21:43

WHEN AS A seminarian I went through a really rough patch, I went to meet with a wise Holy Cross sister. After she listened to my tale of woe, she smiled and said, "Well, because of this struggle that God has sent you, you will finally come down off your moral high horse." I was stunned. Only much later did I see that I had not yet learned to rely on God. I was blind to my pride and self-righteousness.

Jesus' words must have stunned and offended the religious leaders of his day. They were the keepers of the truth and the servants of God. Yet Jesus saw in them what they did not and could not see in themselves: their own pride and sinfulness. By trusting in their own abilities—in their holiness and goodness—they had closed themselves to the channels of God's grace.

To get at our own sinfulness and darkness, we must ask ourselves, "What would I like to hide from others?" If we are honest, the answer will unsettle us, but the humility born from that self-knowledge is the only antidote for pride and self-reliance. And it is only in humility that we let God use us as he sees fit, and thus produce fruits for the kingdom.

Patrick Neary, C.S.C.

Saturday, Week Two

[The prodigal] set off and went to his father. But while he was still far off, his father saw him and was filled with compassion; he ran and put his arms around him and kissed him.

—Luke 15:20

IN MORE THAN thirty-five years as a penitent and fourteen as a confessor, I would say that most of us can readily identify with the prodigal son. Like that wayward soul, we have foolishly indulged our appetites until there's nothing left but emptiness and misery. And like him, we have longed to return home. The sacrament of reconciliation offers us that homecoming, but we worry so much about how we will be received. Just as the prodigal son did, we plan our return and rehearse our defense, but we fear that we are too far gone or that we might not be believed.

If only we could remember that Jesus told this story not to remind us of our own pitiful behavior but to manifest the love of the Father, we would spare ourselves a lot of aimless wandering. The Father has been waiting for the slightest hint of our return. He does not wait to hear excuses; he does not peer into our eyes for true remorse. He is too busy in the embrace of our homecoming, too caught up in his joy over our return—he doesn't care why. As he lavishes his love and joy on us, we are left wondering what took us so long.

David J. Scheidler, C.S.C.

Sunday, Week Three

"Everyone who drinks of this water will be thirsty again, but those who drink of the water that I will give them will never be thirsty. The water that I will give will become in them a spring of water gushing up to eternal life." The woman said to him, "Sir, give me this water."

—John 4:13–15

MY MOTHER DIED last year. While the first weeks afterward were very busy with all the responsibilities following a death, soon I began to plunge into profound grief. In the midst of my anguish, I realized I was facing another loss. Yes, I missed the physical presence of my mother and would do so for the rest of my life. The depth of the mourning, however, was also about my own identity. With her dying I felt lost, alone in a desert, questioning who I was and thirsting for answers.

As I reflect on the Samaritan woman in light of my experience after losing my mother, I realize that she too had a very specific identity.

She belonged to a certain culture that told her who she was. But her encounter with Jesus made her question these beliefs while offering her something vastly different.

We don't know what happened to her after this encounter. And yet, as we ponder what might have become of her, we are faced with our own choices. If we are truly thirsting for new life, we have to be willing to walk the solitary journey through the desert of loss and enter into the demands of a new relationship with ourselves and with our God. We don't go searching for these crosses. They come into our lives at providential moments, at times of divine intervention.

This Lent, we too are at the well, invited by Jesus to draw our identity more deeply from the living God. It remains but for us to thirst for a spring of water from the hand of God.

Mary Kay Kinberger, M.S.C.

Monday, Week Three

*As a deer longs for flowing streams, so
my soul longs for you, O God. My soul
thirsts for God, for the living God.*
—Psalm 42:1–2

I ENTERED HOLY Cross because I thirsted for
God and believed that my thirst would be
quenched in religious life and the priesthood.
Even though I have felt God's presence and
drunk from his life-giving stream in Holy
Cross, I have found that my thirst not only
continues, but actually grows even stronger. Yet
rather than being a source of fear and despair,
this continued and growing longing for God
brings me great faith and great hope in the
future.

I now realize that it is not so much what
quenches our thirst for the Lord, but what
whets it that leads us even more to God's will in
our lives. A growing longing for God is often a
sign that we are in the right place and the right
vocation, rather than the wrong one. It is that
yearning that drives us to know, love, and serve

God ever more in our lives and to work so that he is known, loved, and served ever more by others in their lives. It truly is a beautiful and blessed thing never to stop thirsting for God. In him alone will we receive the fullness of life for which we thirst.

Alfredo Olvera Ledezma, C.S.C.

Tuesday, Week Three

Make me to know your ways, O Lord; teach me your paths. Lead me in your truth, and teach me, for you are the God of my salvation.

—Psalm 25:4–5

A FEW YEARS ago, I was at the reunion of one of the classes I had taught at our Holy Cross secondary school in Taunton, Massachusetts. During the social hour, a former student came over to express his gratitude to me for teaching him the four cardinal virtues. He promptly named them as prudence, justice, fortitude, and temperance. He said it had been his goal to live these virtues ever since my class. I was astounded. Taunton was one of my earliest assignments, and this was his fiftieth reunion!

All of us who instruct and mentor young people, whether as teachers, parents, coaches, grandparents, or godparents, are privileged with a great opportunity to influence them as their minds and hearts develop and they determine what ideals will guide their lives. At our best, we are pathways of grace as God seeks to show them his ways and lead them in his truth. And yet, if we are to teach them God's ways, we must first ask God to teach us. For it is only in following the path of the Lord in our lives that we ourselves and all those we guide can come to discover God as the God of our salvation.

Renatus Foldenauer, C.S.C.

Wednesday, Week Three

Take care and watch yourselves closely, so as neither to forget the things that your eyes have seen nor to let them slip from your mind all the days of your life;

*make them known to your children and
your children's children.*

—Deuteronomy 4:9

In 1970, Graham Nash of Crosby, Stills,
Nash and Young wrote a song called "Teach
Your Children." It includes the haunting lyric:
"Teach your children well, their father's hell
did slowly go by." How often do we resist
remembering the things that our eyes have seen
because some of these memories may be painful? I know that I myself at times have wanted
to forget. Memories can be healed by God
with and through the help of others, although
it may be a great risk to uncover and confront
the pain. But the even greater risk may be for
us to forget!

God, in his Divine Providence, allows all
our experiences, even our crosses, so that we
may learn and grow in love and holiness. They
are all the stuff of grace. If we search for God's
good in the experiences of our lives, we can
learn from God directly. And if we can come
to discover God's good in the sorrows as well
as in the joys of life, then we become people
with hope to bring. This wisdom, born of our
painful memories, is the type of wisdom to

make known to our children and our children's children—to teach them well.

John Paige, C.S.C.

Thursday, Week Three

"Every kingdom divided against itself becomes a desert, and house falls on house."

—Luke 11:17

WHEN JESUS WARNS about a *divided* kingdom, I like to focus on what happens in a *united* family. An Ethiopian proverb says, "When spider webs unite, they can tie up a lion." That is what I have experienced here in Uganda with our Holy Cross family of sisters, brothers, and priests who have united their "webs" over the past forty years.

I think of Holy Cross Lake View, the secondary school we founded in a poor village near Lake Victoria. Through the united efforts of many dedicated Holy Cross religious and lay teachers, it has become a miracle school. Not only have the students succeeded, receiving recognition nationally, but the witness of our Holy Cross charism of unity has spoken volumes to students, parents, and many others.

What greater gift could we in Holy Cross give to the people of Africa who live in countries plagued by war, corruption, disease, and tribal conflicts than to live as one family regardless of nationality, tribe, gender, or age? And what greater gift can any of us give to the communities in which we live, so often torn by division as well, than to unite our webs and work together for God's kingdom? There simply isn't one.

Mary Louise Wahler, C.S.C.

Friday, Week Three

"The first is, 'Hear, O Israel: the Lord our God, the Lord is one; you shall love the Lord your God with all your heart, and with all your soul, and with all your mind, and with all your strength.'

The second is this, 'You shall love your neighbor as yourself.'"

—Mark 12:29–31

THESE WORDS OF Jesus are not just directed to Israel; they are directed to each of us. Yet in our brokenness, how can we ever love God with such oneness of heart? We need to let the Lord refashion us from the broken, scattered pieces of ourselves, because in God alone are we made whole, made one as God is one. Then in God we can recognize ourselves as daughter or son to God and brother or sister to our neighbor. Then in God we can value our interconnectedness with all creation. Then in God we can love life enough to protect it and to call it from death to resurrection. Then in God we can see Jesus in the unloved and rejected of society, even in those who seek to disempower us.

This is the difficult yet blessed path of the saints. It is the path of being fashioned anew by God again and again so that we may love as God loves. And it all starts with hearing Jesus' words in our own hearts. "Hear, my beloved one, you shall love. . . ."

Kesta Occident, C.S.C.

Saturday, Week Three

Let us know, let us press on to know the Lord; his appearing is as sure as the dawn; he will come to us like the showers, like the spring rains that water the earth.

—Hosea 6:3

I WAS IN my room enjoying a cup of tea. As my hands surrounded the cup, savoring its warmth, I looked profoundly at them. I began to contemplate how our hands are a sign of the transcendence of the human being. With our hands we greet and make contact with one another. In that way, we realize that we are standing before another person, and although we are different, we are equal in our humanity.

It is a beautiful sign teaching us that we are not to exhaust ourselves on ourselves, but that we are created to encounter all of creation. We live this encounter for the sake of Love, not merely to exist. Christ calls us to go out, encounter, and embrace the "other" among us, for he or she is no longer "other" but our neighbor. And we come to know Christ in our daily lives precisely by looking into our neighbor's eyes and discovering that in this unfamiliar yet concrete face is the face of Christ. Then, moved by him who is Love, we embrace our neighbor. This embrace is like the spring rain that waters the earth and produces new life, for in it we achieve transcendence.

Rodrigo Valenzuela, C.S.C.

Sunday, Week Four

[Jesus] spat on the ground and made mud with the saliva and spread the mud on the man's eyes, saying to him, "Go, wash in the pool of Siloam" (which means Sent). Then he went and washed and came back able to see.

—John 9:6–7

I HAVE OFTEN wondered if this man with mud on his eyes, finding his way to the pool of Siloam, ever thought, "This will never work." Still he went to the water, trusting Jesus' word.

He did not even ask a question; he simply went and washed. I have also wondered what he thought after washing and seeing for the first time in his life!

I have never experienced physical blindness, but I have trusted what others could see though I could not. When I was first assigned to the ministries of training new members in Holy Cross and later to helping lead our community, my initial reaction was surprise and concern. I thought that I would stumble along, not sure that I had the necessary gifts. Yet I listened and trusted those who told me I did have the gifts because they had seen them in me. Both ministries have proven to be graced and transformative experiences in my life. I have never forgotten the simple trust that enabled me to wash away the mud of doubts and see those gifts.

Each of us has gifts from God's own Spirit that can be used to serve and support others, to affirm and assist them. Having those gifts, however, does not mean that we will always see them in ourselves. Sometimes we need to be sent to use them, trusting those who are sending us, relying on their vision of what we are capable of doing. Then our eyes will be opened, not only to gifts we had never seen, but also to how much more we have yet to discover and see about this God who loves us.

Joel Giallanza, C.S.C.

Monday, Week Four

For I am about to create new heavens and a new earth; the former things shall not be remembered or come to mind. But be glad and rejoice forever in what I am creating.

—Isaiah 65:17–18

THERE IS A tattoo parlor across the street from our Holy Cross parish in Colorado Springs. On Saturday nights, church folk and leather-clad bikers compete for parking spots on the street. One evening before Mass, I noticed a young fellow—maybe twenty—coming out of the tattoo parlor. His two buddies were waiting for him, eager to inspect their friend's newest tattoo. He took off his shirt to show them. On his back, from shoulder blade to shoulder blade and from neck to lumbar was a beautifully etched Celtic cross. The word "Forgiven" was etched above it and the words "No More Pain" were etched below it. It struck me as a profound prayer, a mark of unassailable hope akin to what we Catholics mark our bodies with upon entering and departing churches. We, like that tattooed young man, mark our bodies with the Sign of the Cross and, like him, take as gospel truth that what was promised through the prophets so long ago has been fulfilled. When it comes to our sins, God has a gracefully shallow memory. His judgment is always mercy.

Patrick Hannon, C.S.C.

Tuesday, Week Four

Jesus said to him, "Stand up, take your mat and walk." At once the man was made well, and he took up his mat and began to walk.

—John 5:8–9

DURING MY EARLY teen years, I went through a period of poor posture and rounded shoulders. I recall my mother's frequent admonition to "stand up straight!" I was perfectly able to do it; it was simply that I'd grown comfortable in my slouch.

But after thirty-eight long years the man at the pool could not stand up straight by his own efforts. The rush of healing grace through Jesus, however, brought him to his feet. Jesus was always raising people up to their full measure of life. He recognized their capacity and called them gently to be more. He also stood up for people who couldn't do it on their own, especially the poor, the outcast, and the marginalized.

At times, we too sense subtle inner stirrings that call us to a change of posture. We've grown too comfortable and become complacent in our ways. We wonder who or what will bring us to our feet. And then, as if by divine orchestration, some person or situation demands of us a response beyond our comfort zone. And once more, grace providentially squeezes its way into the crevices of our souls and we, too, stand tall again.

Mary Ellen Vaughan, C.S.C.

Wednesday, Week Four

Can a woman forget her nursing child or show no compassion for the child of her womb? Even these may forget, yet I will not forget you.

—Isaiah 49:15

WE WERE IN tears that night as we recounted our sad experiences of trying to bring comfort and encouragement to desperate people that day. The previous night we had been stunned as we listened to the dispassionate voice of a government official telling the Peruvian people that the next morning they would find that the cost of bread had quadrupled, as had the price of rice, flour, kerosene—everything! One of our neighbors had only enough money that day for one boiled potato, which she cut in four pieces for her four children. She kept nothing for herself. That was all the family had to eat that day.

I do not know whatever became of that mother and her children, but I do know that she taught me what it truly means to give all. In her tender and selfless love for her four children, I caught a glimpse of the face of God, who as our loving, vigilant mother keeps absolutely nothing to herself and is always ready to give all for her sons and daughters. Such generous, motherly love is, indeed, the love our God has for us.

Maryanne O'Neal, C.S.C.

Thursday, Week Four

[Our ancestors] forgot God, their Savior, who had done great things in Egypt, wondrous works in the land of Ham, and awesome deeds by the Red Sea.
—Psalm 106:21–22

JUST AS I was beginning my tenure as executive vice president of Notre Dame, my parents were brutally murdered. For a period, God seemed so very distant and uninvolved in my life. I could not get over the burden of wondering: "How could this happen? How can I do what needs to be done while my sadness and anger are so prevalent?" And yet through prayer and reflection on what I believed about a passionately loving, caring God, my faith was eventually strengthened more than ever. Remembering God was ever-present made possible what would have otherwise been impossible.

I realize more now that whenever I forget how God has blessed me or begin to think that I alone am in control, my life becomes empty. On the other hand, when I remember the great things God has done for me, I am able to trust God and let him direct my life, making it meaningful and fulfilling. And so it is that the more we sear God's loving presence into our memories in the good times, the easier it is to turn to God in the bad times. Then we will not forget, but remember that God is there.

E. William Beauchamp, C.S.C.

Friday, Week Four

The Lord is near to the brokenhearted, and saves the crushed in spirit.
—Psalm 34:18

I MET TONY in my ministry with people with AIDS. His terrible physical pain seemed drowned out by the pain of his crushed spirit. His feelings of emptiness and remorse over a wasted life only deepened as death approached. He had not seen his mother for nine years due to shame, homelessness, and addiction. His one dream was to see her and beg forgiveness. I felt so helpless, but I called her anyway. Could I hope for a miracle? Despite living 250 miles away, she arrived the next day. I had barely begun to prepare her for how Tony would look when he rushed in, knelt at her feet, and, crying uncontrollably, said, "Momma, I am gay. I have AIDS, and I'm dying. Will you . . . ?" Before he could finish, his mother pulled him into her arms, saying she had known all of this in her heart and that she loved him so much. While they held each other and cried, they celebrated a life now made whole through forgiveness.

In Tony I witnessed how the Lord, indeed, is near to the brokenhearted and saves the crushed in spirit. In Tony I witnessed a living psalm. God's word is coming to life all around us, every day. We just have to meet it. We just have to meet Tony and all the other people through whom the word of God is being revealed in our midst.

Linda Bellemore, C.S.C.

Saturday, Week Four

O Lord my God, in you I take refuge; save me from all my pursuers, and deliver me.

—Psalm 7:1

ONE APRIL AFTERNOON in 1994 in Butare, Rwanda, the violence erupted with the terrifying sound of gunfire. People started to flee in panic as the *Interahamwe*, a militia of ethnic Hutu, hunted down and killed Tutsis. Many came looking for refuge in our house. As the days and the violence wore on, more and more people came, many of them wounded and starving. We gave them shelter, and for this my fellow Holy Cross brothers and I were harassed and beaten. Some of us were even killed. It was the most terrible period of my life. There was nothing we could do but take refuge in God, so we decided to have adoration of the Eucharist every day, and we invited those innocent people who had taken shelter in our house to join us. During that time of prayer with our Lord, I looked for inner peace and prayed for my country.

I suffer to this day from what happened. Even though I am now far away from Rwanda, I still pray for my brothers who died in the genocide as well as for those of us who survived. I believe to this day that it was God who saved and delivered me. When there is nothing we can do, we can always turn to God, for God is always our refuge.

Donat Kubwimana, C.S.C.

Sunday, Week Five

[Jesus] cried with a loud voice, "Lazarus, come out!" The dead man came out, his hands and feet bound with strips of cloth, and his face wrapped in a cloth. Jesus said to them, "Unbind him, and let him go."

—John 11:43–44

MATT WAS A beloved patriarch of an extended Italian family and a cherished lifetime member of a parish where I served as pastor. He was the one on whom everybody depended, so when he suddenly had a stroke and then died, family and friends were in shock. No one, but especially his family, could adjust to life without him. They could not fathom their lives without his goodness and humor, without his generosity and laughter.

Like Matt's family, most of us struggle to envision how we will live without a cherished loved one who has died. That struggle is a natural part of grieving, yet if we are not careful, we can hold on to what *was* so tightly that we become incapable of living what *is* here and now. When we hang on for too long to a loved one who has passed away, our own lives begin to pass us by. We bury ourselves alive in tombs of our own self-pity and grief.

To those of us still grieving the loss of friends or family, Jesus is clear: "Unbind them, and let them go." Yes, sorrow can overwhelm us, but Jesus invites us to find comfort in the hope that takes us beyond the cross of death. He calls us to remember that death does not have the final word. While death is the door that closes to life on this earth, it is also the door that opens to the glorious life prepared for us in heaven. Unbinding our deceased loved one frees us to live and enjoy life here and now, which is what our deceased loved one would want for us. It is time then that we too accept Jesus' call to come out of our own tombs and get on with living—for us and for them.

Tom Lemos, C.S.C.

Monday, Week Five

"Woman, where are they? Has no one condemned you?" She said, "No one, sir." And Jesus said, "Neither do I condemn you. Go your way, and from now on do not sin again."

—John 8:10–11

WHY DO WE sometimes see ourselves, even in this great season of forgiveness, as unforgiven? Even after receiving ashes on our forehead, striving to keep Lenten promises, and emerging from the confessional—why do we at times still carry a burden of guilt? Perhaps we fear, despite the priest's absolution, that God still condemns us. To cast out this fear, Jesus proclaimed to the woman caught in adultery, "Neither do I condemn you." And he says to each of us, "I know you and forgive you completely." Perhaps we believe in God's mercy, but still dwell on some past sin. To drive away this temptation, Jesus orders, "Go your way. My mercy overrides your judgment. Move into the future I prepare for you." Or perhaps we worry we'll slip into the same sins all over again. To confront that concern Jesus commands, "From now on do not sin again." He does not guarantee we'll instantly succeed, but he demands we always trust and always try. He tells us, "Take courage from my love. Do not begin your new life in fear. Believe that ultimately my grace will overcome all sin." We dare to hope for so great a forgiveness, because we dare to believe in so great a savior.

Charles McCoy, C.S.C.

Tuesday, Week Five

The people came to Moses and said, "We have sinned by speaking against the Lord and against you; pray to the Lord to take away the serpents from us." So Moses prayed for the people.

—Numbers 21:7

PRAY FOR ME. As a parish priest, I hear this request daily. In my own ministry and faith journey, I often make that same, humble request of others. No matter who we are, when we face difficulties, big decisions, or important situations, we frequently ask others to pray for us. And often we'll seek out particular people, whether because they best understand our specific need or because they just seem close to God.

Fortunately, we have access to a vast number of people always ready to pray for us—the Communion of Saints. The saints are people who know what it's like to be a Christian in a complicated world. They have experienced the same trials that we endure and have found hope in the Cross of Christ. God knows that sometimes we need some help living out our faith, so he gives us the example of thousands of holy men and women to lead us. With so many faith-filled people to guide us, surely one of them understands what we're experiencing right now and is simply waiting for us to ask for his or her prayers.

Stephen Lacroix, C.S.C.

Wednesday, Week Five

"If you continue in my word, you are truly my disciples; and you will know the truth, and the truth will make you free."

—John 8:31

A FIRST-YEAR TEACHER in the ACE (Alliance for Catholic Education) program, struggling to keep up with the demands of her students, parents, administration, and housemates, was at wits' end. In desperation, she called her mom claiming she could not continue. She was a failure. She was not teaching her kids and was at the breaking point. Her mom listened and then asked her to say one thing she was grateful for that day. After a long, stubborn silence, the mom said, "I am not hanging up until you share one thing for which you were grateful today." Finally, the teacher relented: "The end-of-school bell!"

Over the following months, the young teacher continued to call her mom every day until this practice of giving thanks became her own. Through her growing gratitude, she was drawn out of herself and more deeply into the lives of others and the life of God. The truth she discovered—and that we are all offered—is that God is always present to us and working within us. It is just that we sometimes have difficulty recognizing it. Yet a spirit of gratitude leads to freedom of heart, then to a freedom to love others, and then ultimately to union with God.

Sean McGraw C.S.C.

Thursday, Week Five

"I will establish my covenant between me and you, and your offspring after you throughout their generations, for an everlasting covenant, to be God to you and to your offspring after you."

—Genesis 17:7

THE COVENANT OF God throughout the generations reminds me of the many religious who have gone before me in Holy Cross. Since my first funeral as a seminarian, that of Brother Austin Guenther, I have kept the "death cards" of the men in our community who have died. Some friends give me grief for collecting these cards like the baseball cards I used to collect as a kid. These cards remind me, however, of the fidelity and example of those who have gone before me. Surely they were sinful and broken, but in their own ways they were good, holy, and inspiring as they strove to remain faithful to their part of the covenant with God. They made it to the end with the initials "C.S.C." behind their name—no small accomplishment these days or at any time. In that sense, they are heroes to be remembered, revered, and emulated. Inspired by these deceased Holy Cross religious and by all of our deceased loved ones who have been examples of fidelity for us, we, too, hope to be faithful to our end of the covenant as God is surely faithful to us.

John Herman, C.S.C.

Friday, Week Five

*In my distress I called upon the Lord; to
my God I cried for help. From his temple
he heard my voice, and my cry to him
reached his ears.*

—Psalm 18:6

IN THE CHILE of Pinochet in 1975, I was held
incommunicado in a detention center called
Cuatro Álamos. Even though I was separated
from other detainees and denied contact with
the outside world, I didn't feel alone. At night,
from the upper bunk of my cell, I could see in
the distance the lights from our neighborhood
of Peñalolén, and I knew the people there were
praying for me. I could almost physically feel
their support. It was a powerful experience of
our interconnectedness as members of the Body
of Christ, and it empowered me to maintain a
peace that surprised my captors, even during
the interrogations. Only later, in exile, did I
learn the true extent of the prayers that had
sustained me as I met people from around the
world—some of whom I had known, others I

had not, some Catholic, others from different religions—who told me, "We were praying for you and the others in prison."

From my experience, I know that even now, at this moment, we can reach others in prisons, in beds of sickness, and in distant places. We can help people we know, and others we don't know, who need our spiritual solidarity. Through our prayers, we can be God's answer to their cries.

Daniel Panchot, C.S.C.

Saturday, Week Five

"My dwelling place shall be with them; and I will be their God, and they shall be my people. Then the nations shall know that I the Lord sanctify Israel, when my sanctuary is among them forevermore."
—Ezekiel 37:27–28

OVER THE YEARS that I worked in Canto Grande, a slum neighborhood of Lima, Peru, many people came to visit me. I was always struck by their questions about how I could work in such a place. The slum is located on a dry, dusty, rocky terrain. To the superficial observer, it looks like a chaotic, hopeless, dead-end place. That could not be farther from the truth. It only takes a few days there to see the hope that animates the residents' tenacious struggle for a better life as well as the deep faith that sustains them.

God promises to dwell with us and to sanctify our abode. There is no place, no life where that promise cannot or will not be fulfilled, yet it takes eyes of faith to see it and a trusting heart to allow God's work to progress in our midst. As Christ's disciples, we are sent as educators in the faith to the people whose lot we are to share. We go, however, not so much to bring God's presence as to help people to discover and affirm a presence that is already there so that it can grow and flourish.

Arthur J. Colgan, C.S.C.

Palm Sunday

[Jesus] threw himself on the ground and prayed, "My Father, if it is possible, let this cup pass from me; yet not what I want but what you want."

—Matthew 26:39

ACCEPTING THE FATHER'S will, Jesus became obedient to death. Throwing himself to the ground was a prayer in action, placing himself before God and expressing his complete abandonment to the Father. Jesus' surrender on the Cross was the ultimate sacrifice; he entrusted his spirit completely to God. But it was not just an isolated moment; it flowed from a continuous, practiced disposition of dying to himself and living for God.

As we begin Holy Week, we recall that for us too there is dying to do on our way to the Father. In practicing obedience—whether it is the obedience of religious to the will of their superiors, the obedience of parents to the needs of their children, or the obedience of Christians to the teachings of the Gospel—we acknowledge that there is a larger plan, a greater good, beyond satisfying our own desires. While we may occasionally chafe under the burden of serving another's will and of the little daily dyings, we know that we must all eventually respond, with much more at stake, to the demands of death, our inescapable destiny. Surrendering ourselves while still on the road of life robs death of its tyranny and makes both our life and death meaningful. But this graced surrender does not come easily. Dying along the way takes practice. Holy Week gives us a new opportunity to acknowledge that we need to be saved, especially from ourselves. Positioning ourselves with Jesus before his Father, we seek, like Jesus, to abandon ourselves to God and thus find true life in him.

Richard Critz, C.S.C.

Monday, Holy Week

Mary took a pound of costly perfume made of pure nard, anointed Jesus' feet, and wiped them with her hair. The

*house was filled with the fragrance of
the perfume.*

—John 12:3

THE MARY IN John's Gospel brings to mind
another Mary with whom I lived and worked
in the Holy Land, not far from Bethany. Sister
Marie, as school principal, flew her country's
flag when religious fundamentalism prohibited
any display of national allegiance. This daring
act attracted the attention of an extremist
group. Several representatives entered sister's
office and threatened her, announcing, "We are
Hezbollah." (The true meaning of the word
"Hezbollah" is "Party of God.") Marie laughed.
Astonished and angered, the group demanded
an explanation. Marie replied that she was
Hezbollah long before they were. The flag
continued to fly. Marie thrived, undaunted.
The men departed, instructed.

Just as these two Marys shared an uncon-
ventional and courageous expression of discipleship, they also provoked a similar reaction
from their audiences: shock, embarrassment,
and condemnation. Jesus, however, defended
Mary of Bethany, and surely his response to
Marie of Beirut would be the same: "Let her

alone." Their stories invite us to reflect on what risks we might make for the sake of love and loyalty in following Jesus.

Maureen Grady, C.S.C.

Tuesday, Holy Week

I said, "I have labored in vain, I have spent my strength for nothing and vanity; yet surely my cause is with the Lord, and my reward with my God."

—Isaiah 49:4

ANYONE WHO TRIES to live faith seriously knows the weight—whether it be irrelevance, loneliness, failure, or the like—that wants to engender discouragement in the heart. For me, after over forty years of ordination and seventy years of life, health is now the weight that my soul must bear. For some six years my body has carried a rare disease whose pattern and outcome are unknown to medicine. I have been forced to walk about half alive. I am a vertical skinny box with protruding arms and legs along with eyes to see. My sensation has closed down so completely that I find myself *in* the world but not *with* the world.

And yet, paradoxically, this unexpected condition has become my greatest blessing since ordination. Discouragement roams about me, but within me my heart is more in God's world, and that makes letting go easier. And in the peace of letting go, a light comes to me and gives a certain firmness of spirit to heart and soul. Indeed, there is always hope, for in our trials, our cause rests with the Lord.

Jaime Irwin, C.S.C.

Wednesday, Holy Week

It is for your sake that I have borne reproach, that shame has covered my face. I have become a stranger to my kindred, an alien to my mother's children. It is zeal for your house that has consumed me.

—Psalm 69:7–9

I HAVE HAD my residential visa in Bangladesh suspended for two years. That was my reward for helping lead the opposition to the widespread use of child labor in the ready-made garment industry. I have received several death threats. Those were my recompense for standing up against the military's forced sterilizations of women in a tribal area. But none of that—neither the suspension of my visa, nor the death threats, nor the prevailing attitude that Christians should be seen and not heard in this predominantly Muslim country—has stopped me from working for the sake of the gospel. For the love of Christ urges me, as it urges all of us, to carry on the work of charity and justice no matter the difficulties or threats.

When we boldly shoulder the work of the gospel, we often discover that we servants will fare no better than our master. But, like Jesus, we also discover that when we are truly consumed with zeal for the Lord's house, there is nothing, absolutely nothing in this world, not even death, that can stop us.

Dick Timm, C.S.C.

Holy Thursday

[Jesus] got up from the table, took off his outer robe, and tied a towel around himself. Then he poured water into a basin and began to wash the disciples' feet and to wipe them with the towel that was tied around him.

—John 13:4–5

HOLY THURSDAY IS a special feast day for any Christian leader, whether business manager, priest, teacher, administrator, or parent. "The kings of the Gentiles lord it over them," Jesus said, "but not so with you" (Lk 22:25–26). In the Holy Thursday liturgy, the priest reenacts Jesus' wordless instruction to the disciples when he bends down, washes, and dries the feet of members of the congregation—a jarringly countercultural message.

In my years of ministry as a priest, a philosophy professor, and a university administrator, I have found two major temptations of which all of us must be wary. The first is the use of our position to serve our own ego or selfish desires. The second is pandering to the wants and whims of those we are called to serve in order to be popular, or at least to avoid trouble. Jesus' call is to avoid both temptations and to give ourselves to serving others by seeking what is genuinely good for them. When I have challenged a student to do better or people in an organization to reach higher, the reaction is often quite negative, sometimes hostile. But these challenges, along with the assistance and encouragement to meet them, can be opportunities for the most genuine expressions of Christian love, free of sentimentality and self-interest. When we have the faith and love to lead in this way, we reenact in our lives Christ's wordless lesson of the washing of feet.

John Jenkins, C.S.C.

☩

Good Friday

Standing near the cross of Jesus were his mother, and his mother's sister, Mary the wife of Clopas, and Mary Magdalene.
—John 19:25

AN AFRICAN DEPICTION of Mary at the foot of the Cross hangs on the wall in my room. Mary's head rests on her son's leg, her arms wrapped around the Cross. A woman stands behind her with her arms on Mary's shoulders, as if steadying her. This picture of the helpless, yet faithful presence of Mary, Our Lady of Sorrows and her companion in the face of death has become an image of my own experience.

First, I witnessed the devastation of dementia as it robbed my mother of the precious memories of her husband's deep love for her. Then, as my father's hospice journey unfolded, all I could do was be lovingly present as I begged God for the strength to stand at the foot of his cross. The compassion of others supported me when I felt weary, unable to do anything to ease my parents' passage through death to the promised new life for which they longed. Now a dear friend has terminal cancer, and there are times when I ask God, "How can this be happening again?"

As years pass we are called again and again to stand in solidarity with those who suffer, to be a compassionate presence amidst the questions and anguish that arise when someone we love is dying or when we contemplate the suffering and death of so many people throughout the world because of poverty and violence. Yet when we stand with those who suffer, wrapping our arms around their crosses, Our Lady of Sorrows stands with us. Like her companions at the foot of her son's Cross, Mary's presence and support steady us, reminding us that no matter how helpless we may feel, God's faithful and compassionate love will sustain us.

Joan Marie Steadman, C.S.C.

Holy Saturday

"Why do you look for the living among the dead? He is not here, but has risen."

—Luke 24:5

WHEN I WAS first ordained a priest, I was assigned to a parish with a large grade school. One day early on in my time there, I was celebrating a funeral Mass when outside on the playground recess began. Peals of laughter suddenly permeated the church as the children began to run around and play games. The sound of such joy outside seemed to clash with the sadness inside the church. I remember wincing to myself, thinking: "We should have kept the kids indoors. Their laughter is inappropriate for the funeral." I looked apologetically over at the family of the deceased and saw not anger but almost a sense of appreciation. Perhaps the sound of children at play in the fields of the Lord was not discordant to them after all.

Our pain and suffering are certainly real, especially when we grieve the death of a loved one. Our faith tells us that when we weep our Lord weeps with us. But our grief, our sadness is never the final word. We know and believe that all that is sad will one day come untrue. Our crosses, large and small, will end in gladness because of Christ's victory over all sin and death. His dying and rising destroyed death forever and assured for us an eternal lifetime of joy. And so the laughter of the children on the playground that day, invading a moment of great sadness for a family, may well have been the laughter of angels saying over and over to us inside, "Trust, trust. The one you mourn is not among the dead, but the living—forever."

Peter Jarret, C.S.C.

Easter Sunday

[Simon Peter] saw the linen wrappings lying there, and the cloth that had been on Jesus' head . . . . Then the other disciple, who reached the tomb first, also went in, and he saw and believed.

—John 20:6–8

IN OVER FORTY years as a Holy Cross brother, I have had the privilege of assisting at the funerals and memorial services of family, friends, students, colleagues, and confreres. Such assistance, often rendered with brimming eyes and numbing grief, has ranged from planning prayer services and Masses to serving as a pallbearer and eulogist.

Publicly, most mourners, including me, readily assent to belief in the resurrection, as most in my milieu are Christian. Privately, however, I have been taken aside on occasion and asked, "Brother, does heaven really exist? Will we really be raised from the dead?" These questions are invariably asked in an anguished whisper, as if the very expression of doubt is damnable.

My response surprises some: I don't know. I have no proof of the resurrection, and yet I do believe. My faith, if woefully weak at times, is rooted in the risen, living Jesus. It's okay to doubt. It's normal to doubt. Indeed, the more we have reason to doubt, the more we have need of faith. In my moments of doubt, like Blessed Basil Moreau, I cling to an abiding hope in the risen Lord. I remember how the disciples themselves had doubts, wondering what the empty tomb really meant and asking to see their resurrected master with their own eyes. Then from my very doubt, by God's grace, springs the faith that when Jesus calls us by name, we will see our risen Lord and brother as do our forebears in the kingdom of heaven. And so it can be for us that this Easter and every day we proclaim in faith: Alleluia!

John Tyron, C.S.C.

Monday, Easter Octave

"This man, handed over to you according to the definite plan and foreknowledge of God, you crucified and killed by the hands of those outside the law. But God raised him up."

—Acts 2:23–24

GOD BROUGHT HIS eternal dream of salvation to fulfillment through the death of his Son at the hands of those within and outside the law. In so doing, God's definitive plan and foreknowledge are revealed: God desires salvation for all in Christ.

Each person lives both within and outside the law of love; fidelity and fickleness touch every heart. While we desire to give our hearts completely in love, at times we are hesitant and hold back. Yet God's plan and foreknowledge are never fickle, only faithful. God's plan embraces us with the foreknowledge of a loving Father who anticipates with joy our reciprocation of his embrace. Likewise, God's plan embraces us with the foreknowledge of a loving Father who anticipates with sorrow our rejection, but with even greater joy our return home.

Knowing where we find ourselves in our lives, God offers us there the life of his Son. Yes, in his loving providence, God seeks to stir our hearts through the presence of a friend, the wonder of creation, the challenge of his word, or the communion of the Eucharist. Indeed, God provides whatever we need to raise us to new life.

Thomas P. Looney, C.S.C.

Tuesday, Easter Octave

*"Go to my brothers and say to them,
'I am ascending to my Father and your
Father, to my God and your God.'" Mary
Magdalene went and announced to the
disciples, "I have seen the Lord."*

—John 20:17–18

RESURRECTION IS A daily event. We live the
Easter experience every day. Sometimes we are
like Mary Magdalene, who encountered the
risen Jesus personally in the garden. At first
she didn't recognize him, but then suddenly
and unexpectedly the veil of faith became less
opaque for her. I still remember when a student
named Erin surprised me with a cake on the
last class day at Notre Dame. In her gesture of
thanks, I saw my many students whose energy
and talents taught me that God is a lavish giver
and made me feel like Mary in the garden.

Other times we are like one of the disciples
who must rely on the words and experience
of another to reveal the presence of the risen
Lord to us. A student named John was such a

witness for me. His peaceful freedom after being diagnosed with terminal cancer culminated six months later with his death on Easter morning. The message of faith and hope he spoke and lived has been with me ever since.

When we live with trust and with eyes wide open every day, Jesus, our risen Lord, comes to meet us again and again, yet always unexpectedly and always as if for the first time.

Mary Louise Gude, C.S.C.

Wednesday, Easter Octave

When [Jesus] was at the table with them, he took bread, blessed and broke it, and gave it to them. Then their eyes were opened, and they recognized him.

—Luke 24:30–31

ALTHOUGH STILL NEW to the priesthood, I have already found that two of the great privileges of my ministry are the ability to preside at the Eucharist and the opportunity to be welcomed into the lives of my parishioners and know their joys and struggles. During every Mass I say, these two privileges converge as I take the host in my hands and break the Bread of Life before the People of God. As I adore the host and look out at the congregation, I recognize Jesus both in the breaking of the bread and in the sometimes broken lives that my parishioners and I live together day by day.

Like the disciples on the road to Emmaus, we walk the path of discipleship. At times we may be downcast, unable to recognize Jesus' presence alongside us because of the pains and losses in our lives. Like the disciples on the road, we need to come to know him in the breaking of the bread. It is then that our eyes are opened to see that it is precisely in our brokenness that Jesus comes to us and gives us new life and meaning.

Stephen M. Koeth, C.S.C.

Thursday, Easter Octave

While they were talking about this, Jesus himself stood among them and said to them, "Peace be with you."

—Luke 24:36

I STILL REMEMBER the moment some twenty years ago when a simple thought arose out of a crisis now long forgotten: "It will be okay." I felt such deep gratitude for that gift of peace. A second thought followed later: "It will *all* be okay." The "all" gave me chills. It seemed a profound assurance about life in a cosmic sense, and I have since found refuge in its remembrance many times. Yet none has been greater than when Hurricane Katrina struck the Gulf Coast, including my hometown of New Orleans, on August 29, 2005.

As I drove through miles upon miles of devastation, hearing the deadly silence left by life destroyed, I shared the despair rampant among the people who had been violently uprooted. These were my people; this was my city. Yet at some point during the aftermath, I came to appreciate even more the depth of those simple words as they echoed in my soul: "It will all be okay." They are intrinsically linked to the simple words of the risen Lord that we hear and hope for at every liturgy: "Peace be with you." Yes, it will all be okay, for the Lord's peace is with us—no matter what.

Gretchen Dysart, M.S.C.

Friday, Easter Octave

"If we . . . are asked how this man has been healed, let it be known to all of you, and to all the people of Israel, that this man is standing before you in good health by the name of Jesus Christ of Nazareth."

—Acts 4:9–10

THE GIRL HAD been severely sick for days, refusing any food except dissolved biscuits. Strange voices different from her own had been heard saying, "We have come to kill you." I went with her brother, who was also a Holy

Cross priest, to visit her in Tanzania. We started praying, asking Jesus to send his Holy Spirit into the girl to cast out all the evil spirits and to heal her sickness. Suddenly her voice changed. She fell wheezing onto the floor. I placed a crucifix on her chest and voices screamed, "We are being burnt. We are going." She then went silent until I woke her. I asked her to walk, and she confirmed she was feeling well. That very moment she ate a plate of food and started serving us. The girl has been well ever since.

Jesus has never changed. He is the same yesterday, today, and forever. If we believe that in the celebration of the Eucharist God changes bread and wine into the Body and Blood of Christ, surely we can, through that same faith, believe that Jesus can still heal as he did in the past.

James Burasa, C.S.C.

Saturday, Easter Octave

Peter and John answered them, "Whether it is right in God's sight to listen to you rather than to God, you must judge; for we cannot keep from speaking about what we have seen and heard."

—Acts 4:19–20

PETER AND JOHN'S arrest would be neither the first nor the last time that Jesus and his followers were in conflict with human law. Jesus' preaching and actions recognized the fundamental dignity of all persons—tax collectors, prostitutes, lepers, immigrants, the poor—persons who were often invisible. Jesus saw them and restored their dignity, and for that, those in power persecuted him.

In our own day, fidelity to the gospel will bring us into conflict with authorities no less than in Jesus' day. Defending life in the womb or life in a jail cell provokes conflict. Reaching out to the immigrant brings accusations of a lack of patriotism. The gospel, however, calls us to respect all human life and to welcome the stranger. In my own parish we have women in crisis pregnancies, families with loved ones in prison, and immigrants from Latin America and Poland. Certainly, there are no easy answers to complex questions. Nonetheless, like Peter and

John, we are to proclaim bravely and zealously the good news of Jesus Christ.

Christopher Cox, C.S.C.

Second Sunday, Easter Octave

Jesus said to them again, "Peace be with you. As the Father has sent me, so I send you." When he had said this, he breathed on them and said to them, "Receive the Holy Spirit."

—John 20:21–22

WHEN WE SIT and pray, we do not just sit and stay comfortable with the way we are. One of the gifts of prayer is the gift of peace. But when we truly pray, we also receive the gift of the Holy Spirit. And the Spirit always moves us to some kind of response as his power changes us and sends us on mission.

In almost a half-century in religious life, however, my experience has been that as powerful as the Spirit is, his promptings are often very subtle. I remember when I was trying to discern whether I was called to return to serve in East Africa. The moment of clarity came not in any powerful, mountaintop experience, but when my spiritual director simply said to me: "When you speak of the people in Uganda, I hear a great warmth and affection. Don't you believe that is where the Lord is calling you?" That was it. In a quiet, gentle way, it all became very clear. I asked my superior for a change, and my address has been East Africa ever since.

My experience then was much like that of Elijah on Mount Horeb. The Lord told him to go up the mountain and he would see the Lord pass by. The Lord though, was not in the strong wind, not in the earthquake, not in the fire. No, the Lord was in the tiny, whispering sound of a breeze. More often than not, it is through such tiny whisperings that the Spirit speaks and sends us forth to continue Christ's mission. Perhaps our mission will not be as dramatic as crossing the Atlantic and carrying the gospel to Africa, but it will require us to leave our comfort zone and go in peace to make God known, loved, and served.

Alan Harrod, C.S.C.

CONTRIBUTORS

Adamson, M., Ash Wed

Beauchamp, E. W., Thurs, Wk 4

Bednarczyk, P., Tue, Wk 2

Bellemore, L., Fri, Wk 4

Burasa, J., Fri, Easter Octave

Colgan, A., Sat, Wk 5

Cox, C., Sat, Easter Octave

Critz, R., Palm Sun

Dysart, G., Thurs, Easter Octave

Dziekan, T., Fri, Wk 1

Eliaona, D., Tue, Wk 1

Fetters, D., Sun, Wk 1

Foldenauer, R., Tue, Wk 3

Giallanza, J., Sun, Wk 4

Gomes, P., Mon, Wk 2

Goulet, J., Thurs, Wk 1

Grady, M., Mon, Holy Wk

Gude, M. L., Tue, Easter Octave

Hannon, P., Mon, Wk 4

Harrod, A., Sun, Easter Octave

Herman, J., Thurs, Wk 5

Hesburgh, T., Wed, Wk 2

Irwin, J., Tue, Holy Wk

Jarret, P., Holy Sat

Jenkins, J., Holy Thurs

Kinberger, M. K., Sun, Wk 3

King, J., Wed, Wk 1

Koeth, S., Wed, Easter Octave

Kubwimana, D., Sat, Wk 4

Lackenmier, J., Thurs, Wk 2

Lacroix, S., Tue, Wk 5

Ledezma, A. O., Mon, Wk 3

Lemos, T., Sun, Wk 5

Looney, T., Mon, Easter Octave

McCoy, C., Mon, Wk 5

McGraw, S., Wed, Wk 5

Neary, P., Fri, Wk 2

Occident, K., Fri, Wk 3

O'Neal, M., Wed, Wk 4

Paige, J., Wed, Wk 3

Panchot, D., Fri, Wk 5

Raab, R. P., Sat after Ash Wed

Scheidler, D., Sat, Wk 2

Schmitz, G., Thurs after Ash Wed

Steadman, J. M., Good Fri

Timm, D., Wed, Holy Wk

Toepp, M., Fri after Ash

Tryon, J., Easter Sun

Valenzuela, R., Sat, Wk 3

Vaughan, M. E., Tue, Wk 4

Vickers, J., Sat, Wk 1

Wack, B., Mon, Wk 1

Wahler, M. L., Thurs, Wk 3

Zurcher, T., Sun, Wk 2

ANDREW GAWRYCH, C.S.C., graduated from the University of Notre Dame with a Bachelor of Arts degree in Government and International Relations in 2002. He received a Master of Divinity degree from the University of Notre Dame in 2007 and was ordained a priest in the Congregation of Holy Cross in 2008. He currently serves at St. John Vianney Catholic Church in Phoenix, Arizona. He and Kevin Grove, C.S.C, co-edited *The Cross Our Only Hope: Daily Reflections in the Holy Cross Tradition* (Ave Maria Press, 2008).